The Pocketbook of Transformation and Transcendence

Karen Cornell, Jane Li Fox &
Marleen Putnam

FIRST EDITION
First Printing, 2008
Cover design by Linnea Armstrong

Cornell, Karen, Jane Li Fox & Marleen Putnam—
          The Pocketbook of Relationships/
Karen Cornell, Jane Li Fox & Marleen Putnam 1· ed.
                p.   cm.
                Includes bibliographical references.
                ISBN:978-0-9797906-2-1
If you wish to contact the authors or would like more information about this book, please contact the authors in care of Triple Eight Publishing and we will forward your request.

Karen Cornell, Jane Li Fox & Marleen Putnam
Mountlake Terrace, WA

pocketbook3@gmail.com

Contents

Acknowledgement

We would like to thank the Universe for giving us the perfect symbol to describe this book. On the cover, you will see the Infinity Symbol with a star in the middle. This continuous loop shows that we are half spirit and half physical, and with no end. Both are connected, one to the other. The star in the middle is where you want to be — perfectly balanced, able to look in both directions. A very good place to be indeed.

— The Authors

INTRODUCTION

One of the funniest books written was penned many years ago by the late Erma Bombeck. The title was, *If Life is a Bowl of Cherries, What Am I Doing in the Pits?* In this, our third pocketbook, we want to show you how to "transform" your life from the "pits" to the life of your dreams. It almost sounds too simple, doesn't it? But here is the point. It really is simple. We are just so used to struggling and pushing against the Universe, that we give up in exhaustion and defeat.

So, where are you in your life? What would you like to change? Where do you want these changes to take you? How are you going to get there?

In this book, we are asking you to assess where you are in your life and what you would like to change (transform) about yourself or your life. Then we are here to show you how to be brave enough to move beyond the ordinary, and the limits of life, so you will be able to excel in your goals. (That is "transcending"!) This book is about getting from "here" to "there" and enjoying the journey along the way.

TRANSFORMATION

1. *Changing in form or appearance.*
2. *Changing in condition, nature or character.*

THE DILEMMA

To laugh is to risk appearing a fool.

To weep is to risk appearing sentimental.

To reach out for another is to risk involvement.

To expose feelings is to risk rejection.

To place your dreams before the crowd is to risk ridicule.

To love is to risk not being loved in return.

To go forward in the face of overwhelming odds is to risk failure.

But risks must be taken because the greatest hazard in life is to risk nothing.

The person who risks nothing, does nothing, has nothing, is nothing.

He may avoid suffering and sorrow, but he cannot learn, feel, change, grow or love.

Chained by his certitudes, he is a slave.

He has forfeited his freedom.

Only a person who takes risks is free.

—Author Unknown

Part One

Transformation

If Life Isn't Working For You, Why Not?

Is your life organized, serene and running smoothly? Or are you multi-tasking yourself into the insane asylum? If you have fallen into the habit of living with fractured energy, it is time for you to stop and take a look at your life.

When your attention is in too many places at once, you have that "fractured" feeling. Your brain is operating on overload and cannot operate at 100% on any one task. This creates chaos and havoc for you and everyone else around you. Now you have created major stress, which in turn affects your job, your relationships, your friendships ... it affects your whole personality.

Have you taken on too many projects because you can't say "no"? Who are you trying to impress? Your boss? Your mate? Your parents? Yourself?

Everyone wants to be a hero. We all want to look good in our own eyes, and we want everyone to love us. The problem with this kind of behavior is when you spend all of your time

doing a hundred tasks a day, you are not ever
focusing on *you* and what your personal needs
may be. The only way we can do the best for
those around us, is to do the best for ourselves.

Is what you are doing bringing you joy and
fulfillment, or is it leaving you feeling frustrated
and defeated? If you are not feeling joy in your
life, you are probably on "auto pilot." It is time
to take back the controls of your space ship and
set some priorities.

So, do you want to soar in your spaceship,
or do you want to hitchhike? It is time to think
about what you are thinking about!

Every thought you have is an energy. It is
creative in nature. If you are thinking lower
thoughts, you are creating lower energy. And
this will bring negative experiences to you over
and over again until you change the way you
think. It may take some work to change your
thinking habits, because we are so programmed
to think in a negative manner. But if you want to
change your life into one of serenity, peacefulness and joy, you must transform your way of
thinking. This means paying "attention" to what
you are thinking, saying and doing.

The first order of business is to pay attention
to your "self-talk." Thoughts are things. They go

out into the Universe, collect "like energy" and bring it right back to you.

The Bible says, "as ye sow, so shall ye reap." That has a much deeper meaning than digging up a field! We can paraphrase that as "as you think, so shall you create your life." In other words, "what goes around comes around." and it all starts with you changing your thinking patterns to a more positive and higher way of thinking.

If a lower frequency of thinking brings you lower, more unpleasant experiences, then changing to a higher frequency of thinking should bring you the experiences that you truly desire. Paying attention to your thinking and consciously changing it will change the decisions you make, change what you are doing, change the people around you, change your response to things and their response to you. It becomes more than just "wishful thinking" that you want your life to change. It puts you back in the pilot's seat as the creator of the changes you want to see happen. This is you taking your personal power back and recognizing that you are in charge of creating your life. This is true personal transformation.

Warning: This may create a few repercussions in your life (i.e., responses from others). Be prepared for the fact that not everyone may understand what the heck you are doing or talking about! For example: some people may be on the same frequency and choose to go on your spaceship, while others may pass and choose to continue to hitchhike! Both are okay, as all of us are on our own path.

The important thing to remember, in the essence of a linear existence, is that each day affects the next. How are you affecting your tomorrow?

Change your "self-talk" from
"I can't, I won't, it doesn't" to
"I can, I will, it does!"

2

IS YOUR MIRROR OUT OF FOCUS?

When you look in the mirror, who do you
see? Do your images of yourself fit who you
really are? When we speak of your reflection
in the mirror, we do not necessarily mean the
freckles on your face! We are speaking more
about the person inside looking out. It isn't the
shape of your nose that is creating your reality.
It is what is going on inside that head of yours
that creates your reality, and that is reflected
through your eyes looking back at you in the
mirror.

Does the person that you see seem self-
confident and secure? Or is the image you are
projecting one of fear, uncertainty, and down-
right panic? In order to find the "real you," it is
necessary to be completely honest with yourself.
That is what we call being "authentic."

Being honest with yourself means you must
examine your own ideas and what is important to you, rather than always trying to follow
someone else's ideas about what is right for you.
Taking on someone else's ideas may not fit who

you truly are. This means you must get to know yourself really well, and this may take a long time and a lot of work. However, the end result can be that you turn out to be a really wonderful person! Remember that we are all a work in progress. The biggest influences in developing a self-image come when we are very young. But as we get older, continuing to operate on other people's ideas and belief systems may not serve you well.

It takes courage to look in the mirror and recognize that you need to make some changes in your belief systems and the way you think. If you have spent a lifetime believing someone else's ideas, you may find it very hard to even figure out who you really are or what you really believe. This is where "choice" comes in. You can make a choice to change who you are, how you believe and the direction you want your life to take.

How do you decide what you want to change? You ask yourself, "What am I doing and why am I doing it?" (We want to insert here that when you decide to make changes in your life, you must be doing it for *yourself* because *you* want to change *your* life. You can't be doing it for your mate, your parents, your friends, your kids, or anyone else. It must be only for you or you will fail.)

In today's world, society puts much emphasis on quitting smoking, being drug free, not drinking, going on a diet, exercising, etc. etc. etc. How many of those things have you tried to do and failed? If you were doing any of those things to please someone else, that is why it didn't work. You can consciously think or say that you are going to do something, but it is the subconscious mind that is running the show, and whatever programs are in there are controlling your actions and outcomes.

Before you start to identify the things about yourself that you need to come to terms with, we would like to say something to you. You are not a physical being trying to become spiritual. You are a spiritual being focusing through a human body. You may not be perfect, but you are unique and extraordinary.

If the cockpit of your spaceship (that is your mind) looks a little complicated to you, try pushing a different button and see where it takes you!

Is Your Life a Broken Record, Repeating the Same Experience Over and Over Again?

Every time you have a thought, you have a choice. The problem is, most of us don't pay any attention to our thoughts. The average person has about 60,000 thoughts a day, and because we don't pay attention, we repeat the same thoughts day after day.

Thoughts are powerful things. Just because you don't say something, the thought still carries energy and has an effect not only on you, but on the whole planet as well. If what you are thinking about creates energy, then it stands to reason that if you are thinking really negative thoughts, you are sending out really negative energy.

Next time you find yourself in an unfavorable situation, ask yourself what you have been thinking about. Because most assuredly, that is the catalyst that brought about the experience. While your energy going out has an effect on everyone, it more immediately affects you. Most thoughts are like old tapes that keep replaying in your head. It is time to take a look at what is on those tapes. The ideas you play over and over in your head have mostly been with you since childhood. How is that working for you today?

The first step in making a change in your thinking patterns is being aware of your thoughts. Your thoughts create your feelings, and your feelings are an internal guidance system. So being aware of how you are feeling will put you in touch with those thoughts that need to be changed.

Personal transformation is internal chemistry, which means you get to choose the tapes (thoughts) that are running in your head. How do you *want* to feel? You get to "choose" positive or negative thoughts. Just be aware that your choices will create positive or negative experiences accordingly. Whatever you get in life is a response to the lowest energy vibration you are putting out. So "up" your vibrations, folks!

If you want to soar high in your spacecraft, you need to drop the "Kling-ons"! Fears, phobias, bigotry, hatred, anger, etc. are all tapes you need to jettison. Replace those tapes (thoughts) with positive ideas, creative activities, pleasant pursuits and love, love, love!

Remember, this is a process. If it took you your whole life to get where you are, it is going to take some time to make some positive changes. Be patient with yourself. You are still a work in progress. Be in love with yourself now. Accept yourself as you are, knowing that you have the power to change who you are and what you believe, with every thought you have.

As you change "your" thoughts, the world around you will change. Not just for yourself, but for all those people around you. Think of yourself as a pebble dropped into a pond. The circles radiate out to the pond's edges. Every thought you have is a pebble radiating out into the Universe. Make sure your thoughts are of love, caring and gratitude.

Your attitude of gratitude provides a great launching pad for blast off!

4

So, What is Stopping You?

If you aren't who you want to be, why aren't
you? Let's try to find out. The biggest thing
stopping most of us is fear. We can hear you
saying it now: "I'm not afraid of anything!" Oh,
really?

Let's name some fears. There is the fear of
being less than perfect. How many times have
you *not* done something because you were
afraid of what other people would think? Your
fear of being embarrassed in front of other
people can keep you from doing some very important things in your life.

There is also the fear of being successful.
Many people feel they "aren't good enough" or
they don't "deserve" success. And of course,
there is the fear of failure. Better to not try than
to fail!

Then we have the fear of not being loved
and admired by our mate, our friends, our co-
workers, our relatives ... it goes on and on.
Sometimes conditioning from an accident or

21

another unpleasant experience keeps us from trying something new. And in today's world, there is an underlying fear of outside influences that could affect our lives and those make us feel unsafe.

There is no such thing as security. Situations and opportunities don't come with guarantees. So you have to overcome your fears and try anyway. Nobody makes a change in their life without taking some sort of risk.

Most of us feel that our lives are rather mundane. But mundane situations can lead to transformation. Try changing a routine or a schedule. Change what you eat for breakfast. Strike up a conversation with someone on the bus or train. It is time to step out of your comfort zone and stop being afraid of the unknown. Dare to be different! Dare to change your ideas. Dare to wear something different. Dare to try a new food. Smile at a stranger. You never know who the person is you are smiling at or helping across the street. Stop being afraid that you won't fit in. Dare to stand out! Smile, laugh, have fun, enjoy life and share your joy with others. Take a chance and make a change and see where it takes you in your life! Stop waiting for someone else to do it for you. They are just as afraid as you are. You are the only one who can make choices and take risks for your life. Straddling the fence doesn't work. So make a choice, take a risk and jump!

*When faced with decision,
decide. When faced with a
choice, choose. Sitting on the
fence will leave you tense,
because you neither
win nor lose.*
        — Author Unknown

5

DON'T PUSH ON THE UNIVERSE, OR KABLOOEY!

It is the job of the Universe to bring you what you want. Life is not meant to be a struggle, but in our society we are programmed to think you can't get anywhere without a struggle. We make countless movies about this subject. We give trophies for it! We enable "struggles" by sympathizing with people and supporting them in their "struggle." What we are really doing is allowing them to be "victims" instead of supporting them in taking responsibility for their decisions and choices.

If your life is not going in the direction you want, then it may be time for *you* to take responsibility for *your* decisions and choices. When you are going in a direction that is not beneficial for you, this may be an indication that you are pushing on the Universe. There is a flow of positive energy that comes from the Universe. (We call it "going with the flow.") When you are going against that flow — that is the KABLOOEY part!

The energy stream coming from the Universe is a stream of well-being that anyone can tap into when they are making decisions. Energy becomes exactly what you put your attention on, but you must be clear about what you want. You can't get where you want to go until you know what you want. The big trick here is you have to be willing to give up the control on *how* you are going to get what you want. There are so many ways to get what we want we can't even imagine them all! Put your attention on what you want and then step back and let 'er rip! The Universe will bring you wonderful opportunities. All you have to do is take advantage of them. Your job is just to trust that the Universe has your best interests at heart.

Go for it, baby!

TRANSCENDENCE

1. *Moving beyond ordinary limits.*
2. *Surpassing; excelling.*

LIVE A LIFE
THAT MATTERS

We convince ourselves that life will be better
once we are married, have a baby, then another.

Then we get frustrated because our children are
not old enough and that all will be well when
they are older.

Then we get frustrated because they reach ado-
lescence and we must deal with them. Surely we
will be happier when they grow out of the teen
years.

We tell ourselves our life will be better when
our spouse gets his/her act together, when we
have a nicer car, when we can take a vacation,
when we finally retire.

The truth is, that there is no better time to be
happy than right now. If not now, then when?

Your life will always be full of challenges. It is
better to admit as much and decide to be happy
in spite of it all.

For the longest time is seems that life is about
to start. Real life. But there is always some
obstacle along the way, an ordeal to get through,

some work to be finished, some time to be given, a bill to be paid. Then life will start.

It is time to understand that those obstacles *are* life!

That point of view will help you to see that there isn't any road to happiness. Happiness *is* the road!

So enjoy every moment. Stop waiting for school to end, for a return to school, to lose 10 pounds, to gain 10 pounds, for work to begin, to get married, for Friday evening, for Sunday morning. Stop waiting for a new car, for your mortgage to be paid off, for spring, for summer, for fall, for winter, for the first or the fifteenth of the month, for your song to be played on the radio, to die, to be re-born, before deciding to be happy.

Happiness is a voyage, not a destination. There is no better time to be happy than *now*. Live and enjoy the moment.

— *Author Unknown*

PART TWO

TRANSCENDENCE

1

Is Your Spacecraft Able To Take You Where You Want To Go?

How is your navigational system working? Is it taking you where you want to go or is it completely out of whack? Before we go any further, maybe we should discuss what makes up your navigational system. We see this system as being made up of four things:

1. Your power of reason.

2. Your thinking processes.

3. Your ability to trust.

4. Your ability to have faith.

Within the power of reason is your ability to discern positive thoughts from negative thoughts. It allows you to determine what will be best for all concerned. This, in turn, determines the outcomes of your thinking processes. Thinking processes are divided into two categories. The logical, left-brain thinker (we call this the Mr. Spock thinker) and the idealistic, dreamy, right-brained thinker (which

encompasses every artist you have ever known).
The easiest way to navigate through life is to
achieve a balance between these two ways of
thinking.

Trust starts with you. You have to trust yourself and your own ability to make decisions and
choices before you can trust anyone or anything
else. When you trust yourself, you are trusting
the power of the Universe as well. We are all
made up of energy and when you trust in the
Universe, you are exhibiting the ability to draw
on that energy whenever you need it.

Faith carries trust a step further. Faith means
believing in the intangible. When you believe in
something that you cannot perceive with the five
senses, but you feel it in your heart, that is faith.
Faith is what you operate on when all else fails!

We are all explorers in this vast Universe,
and how we operate in the face of unknowns
and uncertainties defines who we are and the
depth of our faith in the unseen. As your ability to reason, think, trust and have faith grows
within you, you will have the ability to navigate
your spaceship to higher elevations of consciousness and awareness. (Remember, YOU
are the spaceship.)

"Good thoughts" vibrate at a very high frequency, so with those, we are moving up in consciousness and awareness. This gives us the ability to travel to uncharted territories within our lives.

Leave your old thoughts behind, head for higher thoughts at warp speed, and get ready for your own "new frontier"!

2

YOU DON'T HAVE TO HAVE A NEAR-DEATH EXPERIENCE TO WAKE UP AND SMELL THE COFFEE!

There are many books out about people who have had near-death experiences. They all talk about how their lives were changed. Suddenly, what had seemed so important wasn't so important any more. They shifted into another gear that made their lives more meaningful. We recommend, however, taking some baby steps as you navigate toward uncharted territories. Baby steps are much easier on you and taking one after the other on a daily basis will lead to higher levels of consciousness and a new level of peacefulness.

So what kind of baby steps should you take? First off, follow the things that bring you joy and laughter. If you are smiling and laughing, everyone around you will be doing the same. That is a sharing of positive and loving energy. Go paint a smiley face on your spaceship!

Next, simplify your life. Spend more time taking care of *you* and less time taking care of

your "stuff". (Please see chapter "Stuffology
101" in *The Pocketbook of Prosperity, Peace
and Personal Power*!) "Stuff" weighs you
down. We have it around, pack it up, move it,
unpack it, dust it. It's exhausting!

Develop a minimalistic attitude. "I don't
need more than I really need" should become
your mantra. Having the "best" does not necessarily mean needing "more." The question to
ask yourself is, "Do I own my stuff or does my
stuff own me?"

Another step is taking more care of *you* and
less care of everyone else. We don't mean to
say that you should just walk around admiring
yourself in the mirror and forget about everything else. But there is a tendency for many of
us to take on responsibilities of others that are
not ours to take on. People need to learn to be
responsible for themselves. That includes *you*!
Now be prepared. When you stop being as
available to people as you were before, you are
probably going to be unpopular for a while!
Trust us. This too will pass. As for the friends
who don't come back, great! You just got rid of
some Kling-ons!

A major lesson on this planet is to learn how to experience love, without conditions. Love yourself first! Then share it with others.

We are all on the same spiritual journey here. Let's not make it a Rocky Road to Heaven!

3
Countdown To Blast-Off!

When you are packing for your trip to higher realms, leave your boxes (which are your limiting thoughts) at the recycle bin. Leave your excess baggage (old belief systems that don't work) at the gate. Limiting thoughts and unworkable belief systems will keep you on the ground. It will make you too heavy for blast-off!

Set a goal to raise your consciousness/awareness to a higher level of thinking for yourself. Let go of the negative thoughts that are rattling around in your head. (We know they are there — we've had them, too!) When you make this shift inside, your life will shift outside. As you shift outside, it not only affects everyone around you, but your change in energy will affect the planet in a very positive way.

Now you are on the road to creating a life of peace and harmony. Remember, you cannot be peaceful if you always have to be right! Be willing to let go of total control over "everything." The only control you can have is over your own spaceship!

One more thing.
After blast-off, don't look back
and NEVER look down!

4

FORGIVENESS AND GRATITUDE: THE ONE/TWO PUNCH!

Forgiveness and gratitude are the foundation for just about everything that comes to us. The "attitude of gratitude" simply means you are putting out an energy that says "thank you" for all you have received. Gratefulness is a magnetic energy that will draw more positive experiences to you that almost always guarantees a flight without turbulence!

A major step toward manifesting your "attitude of gratitude" to the outside world, is to do something for someone "just because" — not because you expect something in return. Be grateful to those who make you happy. They are the gardeners who help you blossom. Before going to sleep and when you first wake up, say "thank you" to the Universe. Remember that the energy you are sending out is what will come back to you. Gratitude will bring more positive things into your life than you can possibly imagine.

Forgiveness, like gratitude, is an important step. When forgiving, forgive yourself first. When forgiving others, say "thank you for that experience." Learn the lesson and move on. Not everyone's spaceship is going where you are going. They may only be heading for the moon, and you may be heading for Jupiter!

Cut everyone some slack.
They may not be ready for the
same trip you are ready for!

5

IF YOU CAN DREAM IT,
YOU CAN DO IT!

Living your life is like writing a book.
Every day is a page in the book and you are the
author. You are in charge and making the decisions. If you don't like the way life (your book)
is going, rip out the page and re-write it! Make
some new choices and decisions. You are not
only the author, you are also the editor. Pay attention to the "story" you are writing (living).
Are you living your own story, or are you living
your parents', your old teachers', your pastor's,
or someone else's?

Living your own life (story), rather than a
life someone else has planned for you, is important if you wish to do more than just survive.
The step beyond surviving is thriving! And what
does it take to thrive? It takes action and being
willing to take responsibility for your actions
in order to live life to the fullest. If you want
increased happiness and joy in your life, think
more positive thoughts. If you want prosperity
and abundance in your life, start being grateful

for what you already have. If you want more relationships and love in your life, be willing to give more of yourself and to love yourself more!

Do you see where we are going with this? No matter what, you are still in charge. What happens in your life is strictly up to you. And as soon as you realize this, you begin to thrive. Although we live in an instant gratification society (we want it all "now"!), the big dreams sometimes take a little longer. That doesn't mean you should give up. The Universe is always there to back you up. Limitations are not set in stone. They are usually shown to us through other people who don't want to see you succeed. Set your goals and be willing to step out and take a risk. Believe in yourself and your goals, have patience with yourself and those around you and never give up on the book you are creating!

When you are creating your dreams, give up worry. It is usually worse than the event!

6

THE SUGGESTION BOX: IDEAS TO HELP
YOU ALONG THE WAY

Sometimes in order to decide where we need to go, we first have to decide where we are. The easiest way to do this is to make a list of all the things in your life that are not working for you. We have been telling you all along that whatever you concentrate on is what you will create, so dwelling on the negatives for any length of time is not a good idea. But in order to identify a direction, you must look at your present situation with reality, honesty and acceptance.

Draw the typical "line down the middle of the paper" with your current list of "don't wants" on the left and the "do wants" on the right. The "don't wants" may involve things that are your current reality. (This is where the honesty comes in. Without honesty you cannot have connection with yourself or anyone else.) The "do wants" may seem to you like reaching for the impossible. But if you have a willingness to make the changes in your life that are necessary, and to take the action necessary to make

those changes, nothing is impossible. Once you
have become aware of the contrast between your
two lists, focus on the "do want" side, which is
what you want to create, and the actions you are
willing to take. Now, get rid of that "don't want"
list. It doesn't concern you any more!

The first step in creation of your dreams is
to visualize what you want. A warning: no one
operates well on overload, so it is a good idea to
start visualizing your goals one dream at a time!
It is important to understand that your dream
will manifest exactly as you visualize it. So
don't leave anything out. Write it all down, draw
a picture, take a photograph if that is possible.
Create your dream "exactly" the way you want
it. And then *know*, with certainty, that it is going
to happen exactly as you visualize it!

Once you have got this picture going,
understand that when the Universe takes over,
your wishes and dreams will expand, often
into something much better than you can even
imagine.

What you focus on expands. That is why we
have been so careful to tell you to focus only on
positive thoughts and ideas. Here is a good exercise for you. When going to bed at night, focus

on three good things that happened to you that day. It ends your day focusing on the positive. Be grateful for those experiences and say "thank you." The next day, you will have even more positive experiences. A wonderful side effect of this exercise is that you will sleep more soundly and will have more positive dreams. And you will wake up in a much better mood, saying "thank you" for a fabulous day!

You need to study, understand and immerse yourself in what you want to create, and avoid the things or people who are where you *don't* want to be. Follow only the things, thoughts and feelings that bring you joy. To really make your spaceship go at warp speed, surround yourself continually with what you want to create in your life.

We have a couple of suggestions for you on things you can do to create and maintain positive feelings. Make a Vision Board or Treasure Map. Go through some magazines, newspapers or books and cut out pictures that represent what you want to manifest into your life. Be specific! If you want a GE refrigerator, don't cut out a picture of an Amana! We three want to be on the Oprah show with our books, so we all have

pictures of Oprah on our Vision Boards! Put
pictures of everything you desire on the board.
If you can't find a picture, write it on the board
in big black letters. Don't leave anything out.
Then put the board where you can see it every
day. What we look at and surround ourselves
with is what programs the sub-conscious and
activates the vibrational energy necessary to
make it all a reality.

Another idea is to put a rubber band around
your wrist. Every time you have thought that is
contrary to what you want to create, snap that
rubber band — *hard!* Cancel that thought and
definitely re-word it. After a few days of a red
wrist, you will get the idea!

Affirmations can be really helpful, but you
must do them correctly and consciously. To do
affirmations correctly, you must word them in
a positive manner and in the present tense. You
must word it as if it is happening now. For example: "I have a new house", not " I am going
to get a new house." It must be believable (by
you!) which is the "conscious" part. Believing
what you are saying is paramount to manifesting
your desires.

Write your affirmations down and put them where you can see them. Repeat them several times a day. And *believe* that the Universe is helping you to manifest what you want.

The ideal affirmation: "I am available to more good than I have ever experienced, realized or imagined before in my life."

— Dr. Michael Beckwith,
The Secret

7

BE COURAGEOUS, SET YOUR COORDINATES AND FULL SPEED AHEAD!

Courageous people aren't necessarily fear-less, they just keep on going and going and going – like the Energizer Bunny! Maintaining positive thoughts (because remember – you *are* what you think) is a big step towards being courageous.

We all have a story that we can change at any time. The trick is to be willing to let go of old ideas and ways of thinking so you can create new ideas and soar beyond the mundane. It is not enough to simply *want* your life to change. You must *feel* it strongly and be willing to take the steps necessary to get you where you want to go. We suggest once again that you visualize your goal. *See* yourself enjoying your new self and your new life.

We all need certainty in our lives. The comfort zone of the familiar (certainty) is what keeps us tied to our old lives and doesn't allow us to make changes. Learning to love and ap-preciate yourself and to depend on the Universe,

creates the certainty and stability you need.
That way if all else falls apart, you still have
you! Trusting the Universe is a huge lesson, but
when you can do that, you will have the certainty that you are okay, and life as you wish it to be
is not only possible — but a certainty!

Remember that when you are soaring, everything beneath you seems small and insignificant.
And problems you encounter will be just that:
small and insignificant. Sometimes the simplest
things are the most effective. Try smiling — the
simplest of all. When you smile, you can't
frown! When you smile, it is impossible to feel
bad! How much more simple can it get?

*As your spaceship heads
toward the stars, remember that
YOU ARE A STAR!*

FINALLY . . .

We have completed our three little books and we hope that each one has helped you in your lifelong endeavors. Only you can take your "life journey." We wish you the best and safest of trips. We will see you on Jupiter!

IDEALS

As you think, you travel and as you love,
you attract.

You are today where your thoughts have
brought you. You will be tomorrow where
your thoughts take you.

You cannot escape the results of your thoughts;
but you can endure and learn. You can
accept and be glad.

You realize the vision — not the idle wish —
of your heart; be it base or beautiful, or a
mixture of both.

For you will always gravitate towards that
which you secretly most love.

In your hand will be placed the exact result of
your thoughts. You will receive that which
you earn — no more — no less.

Whatever your environment may be, you will
fall, remain or rise with your thoughts, your
wisdom, your ideals.

You will become as small as your controlling
desire; and as great as your dominant
aspiration.

— James Allen